Race Track Attack Guide

Willow Springs International Motorsports Park "Big Willow"

The Enthusiast's Approach to the High Performance Driving Experience on America's Road Racing Courses

Edwin Reeser, III

Sericin Publishing Company

ISBN Number: 978-0-9841724-1-2

Library of Congress Control Number: 2010906167

DISCLAIMER: The contents of this book are true to the best knowledge of the author. All recommendations are made without guarantee on the part of the author or the publisher. The author and the publisher disclaim any liability incurred in connection with the use of any data or recommendations in this book. In particular, no portion of this book should be taken to suggest or condone the violation of any traffic laws or the practice of any unsafe driving.

Printed in the United States of America

All maps used to illustrate the Willow Springs driving lines were sourced from Matthew Reeser and Kathryn Marcellino. All photos by Edwin Reeser.

A publication of Sericin Publishing Company,
Sericin Management, LLC
Matthew Reeser, Editor in Chief

Contents

Foreword

Having worked with Ed Reeser at Nissan Sport magazine, I know how keen he is for detail. While most of us stumble through motorsports and life (those two inseparable endeavors) relying on our meager talents, Ed is constantly on the lookout for the smallest details. When he turns his attention to each racetrack, his ability to analyze the topography of the circuit, together with his explanation as to *why* each detail is important can be more valuable than gold.

Perhaps just as important is the display of a thinking man's approach to motorsports. In my twenty-odd years of being an active racer, I've witnessed just how critical this aspect of driving has become. Beyond purely technological aides such as state-of-the-art data acquisition, each participant can get the most out of their track day experience by flexing that most important muscle—the one located between their ears—before, during and after the event. And as you read about balancing risk vs. reward through each corner of the track, you'll begin to appreciate Ed's successful approach to high-performance driving.

Beyond that, and even if you use this book to gain greater insight into specific corners or areas of the track you are having difficulty with, Ed offers side notes and suggestions that are well-worth paying attention to. Most of us have learned these lessons through years of bent fenders, busted wheels or worse. I'd suggest reading and re-reading his descriptions slowly to give yourself time to assimilate this information. Once you hit the track, things will happen quickly and you will be faced with making split second decisions that could impact (pun intended) your ability to continue a pleasant day.

Finally, Ed makes the point that no tangible rewards (trophies, points or money) are part of a typical track day or HPDE. But I disagree. The reward that each successful participant takes home at the end of the day is the beautiful, shining car of your dreams. Hopefully, the same one you drove to the track in! And beyond this, it's my belief that each successful lap—driven to the limit of our abilities—transforms us as individuals. Making us more aware of the capabilities of our vehicles and what we can and cannot do, is a priceless experience. Have a great day at the track!

David Muramoto
Editor-in-chief,
Nissan Sport Magazine

Willow Springs International Motorsports Park

"The Fastest Road in the West"

Introduction

Willow Springs International Motorsports Park ("Willow Springs") is located approximately ninety minutes north of Los Angeles, at an elevation of 2,350 feet, six miles west of Interstate 14 at the Rosamond Boulevard exit, west of the community of Rosamond, and a few miles south of the high desert City of Mojave. To the east on this same exit is the famed Edwards AFB, the testing and evaluation airfield for many of the world's greatest military aircraft developed over the past sixty years, and professional home of some of the finest pilots to ever fly.

Willow Springs has three distinct and separate road courses. The self proclaimed "Fastest Road in the West" of Big Willow was created in 1953 as a 2.5 mile oiled dirt surface track, America's first purpose built road course, and today remains essentially unaltered in design as a clockwise circuit. There are also the smaller 1.8 mile Streets of Willow and Horse Thief Mile circuits, which will not be covered in this guide.

This Track Attack analysis will present the driver with a tool to help prepare for a high performance driving lap at the famed "Big Willow" circuit, including track entry and exit procedures.

One should always do a track map study of a circuit before driving the course, view in car videos, look at still photographs of corners and features, and even play a video game simulation, as well as talk to drivers and instructors well experienced with the track. However, none of these will adequately convey the sensory sensations from the extraordinary rush of air and sound from the engine and tires as you hurtle down the front straight, the deceleration pressure on the chest through application of braking before making a corner turn in to Turn 1 that in some modified cars will exceed 100 mph, the lateral g-forces during the long steady arc climbing almost sixty feet in elevation through the 450 foot radius of Turn 2 that subtly tightens and pushes you wide left at corner exit, the plateau charging up hill from Turn 3 that lightens the rear as you transition from Turn 3 to Turn 4 in a sharp eighty foot climb, the conundrum of the Turn 4 "Omega" that has more driving lines than taxis take on Park Avenue, the near weightlessness as you position for a blind apex after and almost four feet below the hill crest of Turn 6, the more than fifty foot elevation drop downhill that has you surging through Turn 7 and into the increasing corner radius of Turn 8, and the gut tightening attendant to the sharply diminishing radius of Turn 9 that has drivers searching for an elusive corner apex, leading to the front straight.

There is thrill aplenty and more than enough speed for any driving enthusiast at Big Willow. Under proper supervision and sponsorship, this course is accessible to most drivers at this writing.

The sign says it all.

Passing to the right, in transition from exit of Turn 9 into front straight. Note sharp rise in elevation at end of straight.

The Track

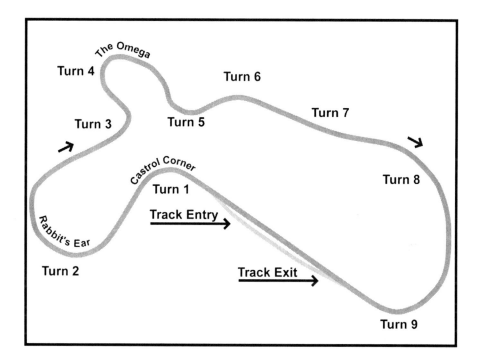

While a chance to drive any car on a race track is usually great fun, that might not be the case at any track absent a well organized event, and the great majority of event sponsors at Big Willow fortunately attend to this carefully. Before selecting your event sponsor to run with at Big Willow, be sure you confirm that they follow a disciplined safety orientation for all drivers. Particularly, check that they separate cars and drivers into run groups that reasonably match expected lap times so that they are in a safe range of not being too greatly variable.

This is a high horsepower track, with typical cars at Big Willow routinely boasting more than 300 bhp, and you may frequently encounter cars with more than 600 bhp. You can have fun with less grunt, but, a stock Miata straining to deliver 133 bhp would be right foot to the floor in top gear for 90 percent of the 2.5 mile circuit, could be in mortal danger of being mowed down by Vipers, Corvettes and other powerful cars at significantly higher velocities (potentially 50 mph speed differential or more) in the same run session (specifically the front straight, and the descent from Turn 6 to Turn 8). Many circuits of comparable length have at least 15 to 20 turns, as compared to 9 turns at Big Willow, (including Turn 7 which probably should not be considered a proper corner for all but the fastest of cars), and thus significantly lower average lap speeds.

Fast closure rates between cars can be dangerous, reducing the time available for the driver in the car being overtaken to pick up with mirrors the overtaking vehicle. (You know what it is like to be in your car parked with the driver side window down and have somebody blow by you at 50 mph. Just the displacement of air by the passing car rocks your vehicle forcefully. Imagine driving 100 mph and have someone pass you at the same difference in speed a skinny three feet to the side. Or similarly, close your eyes and *visualize yourself pedaling on a tricycle in the middle of the fast lane of your local Interstate highway and being approached from behind by a car driving at the legal speed limit!)* That rate of closure causes anxiety for everyone, as the driver in the passing car is uncertain as to whether he has been recognized, and a sudden move by the overtaken car can contribute to a crash or desperate avoidance maneuver at high speed.

Strict "point by" passing rules can reduce some of the risk of high closure rates, but also generate immense frustration from a fast car/driver that must repeatedly slow down to be recognized and then pointed by. Constantly watching your mirrors knowing that you will be overtaken and passed in that environment by several cars every lap is not fun for the driver of the slower car either.

This is one reason why Willow Springs has the Streets of Willow and Horse Thief Mile tracks, where the tight twisty corners and short straights negate much of the advantage of big power, and reward light weight and handling prowess. Some smaller light weight cars with forced induction (turbocharger/supercharger) engines can manage both challenges, at a much lower cost to buy, modify and maintain than many super cars, which helps to explain their great popularity with enthusiasts that want a street legal car that has excellent track performance potential.

(Beginner's note: Most organizations managing a HPDE on Big Willow carefully separate run groups during event registration not only by driver skill and experience, but also by types and capabilities of cars, so that closer comparability of lap times will ensure a day of running that is more safe and fun for all participants. In addition, many enthusiast car clubs that favor a particular make or model of car will reserve track sessions and you may be able to drive with them, subject to their additional participation or membership rules. Be sure when you organize your track day, that you confirm there will be a novice group, with instructors, and no mixing of cars that will result in widely disparate speeds for your group. Also, look into the possibility of a track day at the very popular alternative Streets of Willow circuit before engaging Big Willow.)

Do not be dismissive of the repeated emphasis in this analysis on high speed issues associated with this circuit, as the purpose is to help you know where to focus to manage that speed. Going fast, and going fast *safely,* are not the same thing. Any person, and many trained animals, can get behind the wheel of a powerful car, hold the wheel straight and put the accelerator to the floor. You must not mistake the capabilities engineered into the car to be an extension of your capabilities as a driver, especially with respect to car control at speed. Having a fast car and being a fast driver are two unrelated statements of fact.

Driving this course is terrific fun, but you must recognize and respect the limitations of the track, the car, and yourself with clarity. While most beginners approach track days with the reserve and caution appropriate to reduce risk of mishap, there is perhaps a greater risk on this track for the intermediate and advanced drivers who are pushing the envelope of performance limits for their cars, and their own driving skills, but at higher speeds than they may be used to. Control recovery at high speed is more difficult, and the consequences of lost control to driver and machine more severe, so respect this attribute of speed when driving every course, and especially Big Willow.

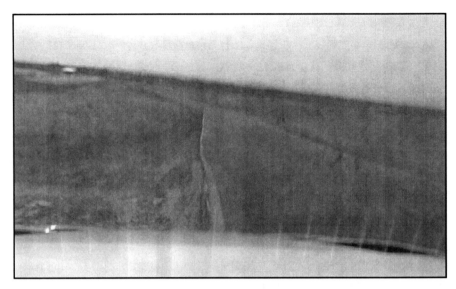

Two wheels off at exit of Turn 6. Cold tires, cold track, cold air on first run of the day; grip is significantly reduced under those conditions.

Always keep your eye on the starter as you line up.

Perspective

Reality Check: Before we get into how to enjoy High Performance Driving Education ("HPDE") and the track notes for Willow Springs, a few words about what this experience is about and its risks.

Many sports involve highly developed skills where you throw, catch, strike, or kick a ball. If you make a mistake the result typically involves a lost point, a change in possession, a replay, or perhaps a lost ball and a "do over" with a scoring penalty, and the game continues. *In high performance driving, you are the ball, and there are no second chances.* Accordingly, driving the "ball" over the fence or into the lake is not an option.

Some sports have a significant potential of serious injury or death if things go wrong. You may do everything right yourself, and still get caught by the mistakes of others or unpredictable events. Mountain and free climbing, scuba diving, sky diving, spelunking, bungee jumping, hang gliding, bull fighting and driving a car, motorcycle or bicycle fast all can have seriously negative consequences, irrespective of fault. If introducing even a moment of inattention to a relatively safer activity, such as crossing a street on foot, can be fatal, (stepping into the path of a bus while reading the morning paper, for example) then it is clear that a moment of inattention in one of the aforementioned activities is potentially more so.

All sports require a detailed level of knowledge and practice to perform well. Striking a golf ball is not an inherently natural series of coordinated actions. Neither is throwing, catching or hitting a baseball, climbing the face of a rock wall, or making a controlled sky diving free fall. HPDE driving is most definitely an undertaking that benefits from serious study of the geometry of tracks, the components and working of your car, the art of driving, safety considerations at all levels, and physical and mental preparation of the driver. You will drive better and be safer if you devote the time and energy to do it right by studying, and practice.

Driving a car is an inherently dangerous activity. Driving a car fast, even under the best of conditions and preparation in a well-controlled track situation, is even more so. A 3000 pound car moving at 60 mph has the potential energy to move a 5,808 TON block of concrete one foot. That car moving at 120 mph has the energy to move a 23,232 TON block of concrete one foot. A speed of 120 mph is not really "fast" in the auto racing world. There are numerous circuits where a street car can reach speeds of as much as 150 mph, or more. ***Big Willow is one of those tracks.*** As kinetic energy increases as the square of speed, twice as fast means four times the energy. If there is a problem on the street or the track, all that energy has to go someplace before your car comes to a stop. If it is dissipated through braking to a smooth stop it is highly desirable, as contrasted with a series of violent roll over strikes upon the ground or against a concrete wall. This is especially true if the concrete wall does not move and the energy is absorbed by the compression of the car with you inside of it.

As you spend more time on the track, the odds of having an unpleasant experience will tend to catch up with you. You will exit the track surface, lose control of your car or have someone lose control of their car in front of you. All people make errors in judgment. All things mechanical and electrical can and eventually will break or fail. Random events can and do suddenly occur. They have happened to me, and all of the other drivers that I know, so there is no reasonable expectation that you will escape this fundamental reality any more than you can defy the laws of gravity.

But you can prepare to make the best of it when bad things happen. Part of the focus of this book is to bring to light how you approach driving and maintaining your car, and whether you may need to consider changing your approach to make yourself a safer driver on the street and track. You may find that track experience can benefit you on the street, keep you out of trouble. Not because you can drive faster than others, but because you are more aware, have developed additional car control skills, and can get the most out of your car and yourself in an emergency.

If you cannot accept the responsibility or consequences of driving on a race track, don't do it. Driving a car under the laws applicable in all licensing jurisdictions that I am aware of is not a right, it is a privilege, and you are responsible to do everything you reasonably can to prevent damage to your car, the cars of others and/or injury to yourself or others. That is just for street use of a car. On a track, the safety and preparation expectations and requirements of most sponsoring organizations is even higher, and the assumptions of the risk that you take for your actions, and those of others, is higher as well. Nobody is forcing you to drive on the track, and certainly you should not allow anybody to persuade you to do it. Thoroughly investigate and study first, and then make up your own mind.

Once you have made the decision that you are going to drive a car on a race track, then it is your responsibility to do it as safely and intelligently as you can, for your own sake and that of those around you. Such care includes your careful preparation of the car, its transport to and from the track, and staging in the garage and pits. It includes your personal skill development and preparation through driving schools and practice in car control on and off the track. It also includes how you enter the track, how you leave the track at the end of your session, how you evaluate the risk areas of the track and develop your plans to deal with those risks.

Be mentally, emotionally and physically prepared for the stresses. The level of concentration required is more intense and sustained than any driving experience you have had on the street, and possibly more than any other experience you have ever had anywhere. The faster you go, the more data you have to deal with, and the less time and distance to deal with it, and however good you think you are, or actually are, sooner or later you will find you are not good enough at some point, in some corner, on some day. That is not good or bad. It is just the way it is.

While you cannot eliminate all of the risks associated with high performance driving, you can do a lot to reduce and to manage risks by proper preparation of yourself and your car, attention to safety at all levels of equipment and driving techniques, and by running with reputable organizations and sponsors of track day events. Please do all of that and more.

The satisfaction that comes from driving a very fast lap derives from an assembly of many little things. It takes time, practice and study to get it right, and patience is a virtue. Fast driving does not come from deciding that you want to drive "fast" and stepping harder on the gas and brake pedals of a car with a big engine. Rather it comes from developing the car control and driving skills to accelerate, turn, brake, shift and balance weight on the car *smoothly and precisely* under a wide array of differing conditions and circumstances. As you improve those skills... speeds increase, lap times decrease, and more importantly your errors should decrease. Slow is *smooth*, and smooth becomes *fast*.

What defines "fast" is what is fast for you. Compared to a horse, you will be going very fast, and for a turtle... even more so. Yet for a beam of light or radio wave you will be virtually stationary! As to other drivers... don't get trapped into that element of competition. It is of no importance that somebody else in a different car is a few seconds slower or faster than you.

If you want to be competitive against others in your driving, and there are many people who do, there are organizations that arrange competitions for "time attack" or racing against the clock versus other drivers, as well as the traditional and popular "wheel to wheel" racing. Those are not HPDE and should not be confused with HPDE. If you want to do that type of competitive driving, get yourself into a proper racing organization and follow their program.

In HPDE, there is no blood, honor or money on the table. No fashion beauties with bouquets of flowers, no gigantic bottles of champagne to spray adoring fans, no poster sized checks for amazing sums of money, await you for being the fastest driver on the track.

The goal is to learn to drive as skillfully as you can as safely as you can at speeds within the capabilities of yourself, the car, and the track under the specific conditions of the day, and then go home at day's end with car and body unscathed.

Stay to left edge during track entry phase. Note on track car on right edge.

Remain on left edge through corner exit from Turn 1.

Track Entry

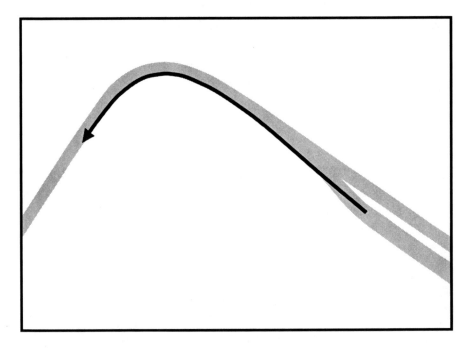

Safety for both the entering car and the cars on track is a priority for every road course, and you need to study and understand both track entry and exit procedure and technique *before* you show up. Given the high speeds of on track cars near the track entry point at Big Willow, special attention must be paid to this aspect of driving the course.

Track entry from the hot pit is at the left edge, near the end of the front straight. Wait for the starter to release you for track entry, and be sure to **look over your right shoulder as you are released by the starter and again before you enter the track** to visually identify cars on the front straight or in Turn 9 that could potentially close on you prior to your exit from Turn 1. With the half mile long front straight distance and speeds high enough to allow some cars to cover that in **less than fifteen seconds**, accurate location of approaching cars and estimating their speeds from the hot pit is too difficult and unreliable through a quick glance in the mirrors alone.

The cars abreast of the start/finish line at the moment the starter releases you are of no concern... they are long gone and through Turn 1 before you can even get to the track surface. It is the cars coming through Turn 9 and entering the front straight at 100+ mph, a half mile behind you that present potential collision risk.

Check your mirrors to reacquire the location and closure rate of any pursuing cars as you merge onto the track, and at a minimum once more before you initiate your turn in to the corner. Cars already on track are approaching the corner entry along the right edge of the front straight at wide open throttle ("WOT") for a fast right to left turn. That means they should be fifty feet away on the right edge of the track when you enter. (But cars are wider than the driving line on a map. They occupy the better part of ten feet in width on each side of the track when you consider the margin of safe space required on either side. That gives you a maximum spacing of 30 feet... ten steps.)

The car entering the track must stay on the left edge of the track surface all the way through Turn 1, and not swing wide right into the path of the fast approaching cars at any time entering through or existing Turn 1 during track entry phase. By following this entry line the only potential point of intersection of two cars should be at the apex of Turn 1 for the approaching car. The approaching car on the front straight should see the car entering the track on the left with adequate time and space to adjust speed and driving line if necessary to avoid a collision with the car that has entered, and thus the track entry is reasonably safe, especially when the standard procedure for the starter holds the entering car until the track presents an opportunity for an entry without an encounter at the corner apex with approaching traffic.

(**Beginner's note:** Remember, once you are merging to this track surface you are **committed** to the entry. The greatest safety to you and to the approaching car(s) is for you to *stay predictable in your driving line and your velocity*. Note that from the start finish line to the entry to Turn 1 you have a significant climb in elevation, so factor that in to your throttle decision. There is about a two foot positive camber working to your advantage from the inside to outside edge of the track surface in this corner as well. Do not wander off line and do not suddenly brake, thinking that doing either will make it easier for the approaching car to get by you, as nothing could be farther from the truth.

The only two things the approaching driver can do is compare rate of closure and driving line with yours in a few seconds of time from about a quarter mile away, project which of you will intersect the corner apex first and by how much, and then commit to a strategy to either pass early, or slip behind you to pass late. Those are the primary two choices.

It is the responsibility of the passing car to pass safely. And do not forget that this strategy may be entangled with his passing or being passed by another car towards the end of the front straight, a dynamic that may have more of their focus on each other than you.

If the choice of the overtaking driver is to pass early, he will go into the corner in front of the entering car and into the apex. If the choice of the overtaking car is to pass late, the pass will be after the entering car crosses the apex, with the passing car then tracking out to the right coming out of the corner apex and then making the pass.

The entering car does not have a widely varied choice of alternative driving lines. Should you as the entering car wander off the proper entry line and out into the driving line of the passing car, you have condemned the passing car to either run into you or, make a third choice if he can react quickly enough, to drive off the course at high speed. If you suddenly brake and his choice was to brake and slip behind you, he could run into you again.

Essentially, by changing track entry line or velocity the entering car is enlarging the zone of potential intersection of the two cars widely, beyond a narrow corner apex point of perhaps a couple of car lengths to perhaps almost the length of the entire corner. So please don't do that.

The best action for the safety of both drivers is for the entering car to get on the line, the only driving line for track entry, and moving as quickly as possible. This is especially true if the entering car failed to pick up the pursuing car visually and is unaware of its approach, or the starter erred and released you when a car was coming down the straight. (Low profile fast moving cars can be easily overlooked. Be prepared for it).

Any element involving human judgment guarantees that errors will be made, not only by you but by every player on the track, both in and out of cars, and they are frequent enough and of great enough consequence to your survival that they must be addressed and provided for in your driving. Just because you were released to get on the track is no guarantee that it is safely clear! So understand what the variables are for each driver and car in the moment, be aware of what is happening around you, leave options for alternative action for both yourself and the other driver, always take responsibility for the safety of your own actions as they relate to yourself and others, and this entry should be safe.

With respect to the actual point of entry on the track, Willow Springs has a reasonably safe entry. Though speeds are high for the on track cars, they have time and space to see the entering cars, and if necessary to make adjustments. And the entering and on track cars are oriented at opposite sides of the track surface. However, every track has at least one point where the driving line of the entering cars and the driving line of the on track cars "blend" together, and this is a primary risk point, though not necessarily the only one. (For example, the entering line proceeds down the left edge of the track after exiting Turn 1 towards entry to Turn 2, while the on track car drifts out to the right edge of the track after exiting Turn 1. The on track car must then transition back to the left edge of the track before corner entry to Turn 2, thus blending the driving lines once more and presenting another decision on whether to pass or slip behind the entering car going into Turn 2.)

What makes the blending of the driving lines potentially confusing is that it occurs going into and through the corner apex of Turn 1. This requires that both the entering cars and cars on track pay careful attention to their respective driving lines. Thus, when coming to Big Willow, you should study and reflect on your driving behavior in both the role of the entering car driver and the on track car driver.

Stay well away from right edge in mid corner segment of Turn 2.

Leaving turn 2 apex, note how outside left edge of track tightens. Also note the exit apex is not on the right edge of the surface, but a car width away.

Turn 1

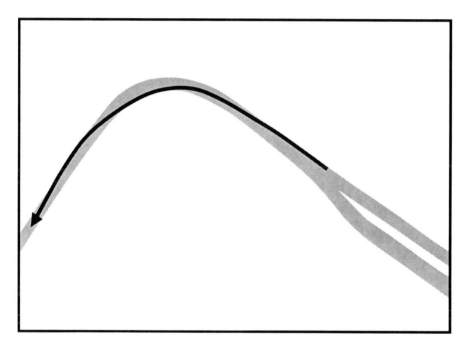

The "Castrol Corner", is a ninety degree right to left corner that can be taken faster than the first impression of many drivers because of the long radius, significant positive camber/banking and the wide track out width to the racing surface on corner exit. The corner is approached from the right edge of the front straight at WOT in top gear for most cars. Unless you are powered by foot pedaling, this is a corner approached in virtually any car at triple digit speeds, and in the high horsepower cars at more than 150 mph.

Check the track entry on your left for any entering cars as you approach the braking zone. Commence your straight braking run and complete your downshifts (if any) before initiating your steering input for turn in. You will have some assistance in your braking as you will be in a subtle elevation climb approaching your corner turn in point. As soon as your front right tire has taken a "set" into the corner, gradually ease on additional throttle so that you can maintain speed and front to rear weight balance through the mid corner phase, and then as you come across the late corner apex be squeezing to WOT and up shift if needed as you complete your track out.

Because the positive camber of the corner rolls away after the apex, the track out point can be difficult to locate visually from before and through the apex point. Therefore you must concentrate on hitting your apex point precisely, and if you do err, make it late on the apex but never early, and holding to your steering lock until you move along your track out driving line far enough to identify the exact location of the right edge of the surface. Otherwise you risk unwinding your steering too quickly and then running out of room and dropping wheels off the right edge at high speed.

As soon as you approach your track out point on the right edge, and confirmed that you will not be running off the surface, be sure to have your head up and picking out your corner entry point for Turn 2 on the left edge of the track, and ease the car across the track under full acceleration down this medium short straight. Check your mirrors for any closing cars before corner entry to Turn 2, and your gauges.

(**Beginner's note:** This is an ideal corner to work on picking a braking inception point, and then gradually work it closer and closer to Turn 1 in small increments, practicing your thresh hold braking technique when initiated at high velocity. ["Thresh hold braking" means the application of the brakes to where you are at the very thresh hold of exceeding the gripping capacity of your tires and locking up the wheels and sliding... it is the application of maximum deceleration available to the car]. Do not trail the brake going into the corner, as this is a fast corner and you want to have all of the available grip for cornering. Only an advanced driver with substantial experience and car recovery skills should do anything other than a straight line braking run for this corner.

Slowing from 90 to 40 mph in thresh hold braking approach to a corner is decidedly different than slowing from 150 to 100 mph for a corner. In addition to the fact that it takes more distance to slow from 150 to 100 mph than it takes to slow from 90 to 40 mph, a small error in driving line or inception of braking is magnified significantly because of the higher velocity and the short time it takes to cover large distances of track surface.

A one tenth second delay in your reaction time to commence braking at 90 mph will place you approximately 13.2 feet beyond your turn in point, while a one tenth second delay in your reaction time at 150 mph will put you almost 22 feet beyond your turn in point. It does not require much imagination to visualize how entering a turn at 100 mph and 22 feet deeper than planned on a track surface that is 50 feet wide on track out is to encounter a panoply of ugly outcomes, with few alternatives that will keep you on the track. If your reaction time is two or three tenths of a second delayed, the multiplier on that distance really puts you 44 to 66 feet off your line, and into the weeds.

You are trying to place the inside front wheel of your car on the apex point, within an inch of that point at most, for a corner. Visualize putting a quarter or nickel on the apex of the corner and consistently just kissing the edge of that coin at 100 mph (with a suspension tuned tightly enough that when you run over the coin you can tell which denomination it is!) To miss your apex point by two feet is even for amateur high performance drivers sloppy beyond words, but you may be able to control the car sufficiently to keep it on the track, at the cost of ruining your lap time (a small price to pay compared to other alternative outcomes). To miss by 22 feet (a one tenth second error) is akin to driving your golf ball out of bounds, over the roof of the nice house fronting the golf course and into their backyard swimming pool.

The answer of course is not to be driving at your absolute "ten tenths" limits of control so that you have some margin for safety and maneuver, irrespective of your level of skill, and to sacrifice speed to keep to a driving line that will touch the corner apex. Concentrate on not upsetting the balance of the car, keeping strict control in your braking run, and carrying straightaway speed deeper to the corner, while still smoothly transitioning the car into and through the corner, and making your apex accurately. Get the "smooth" control first, and the "speed" will follow in due course.)

Turn 1 corner entry is fast, with a late turn in and strong positive camber.

Cover picture. Note positive camber in Turn 1 apex, and track out path of lead car on corner exit.

Turn 1 exit at right edge. Lead car is making transition to left edge position for entry to Turn 2.

Turn 2 entry from left edge is to a driving line that is near mid track.

Turn 2

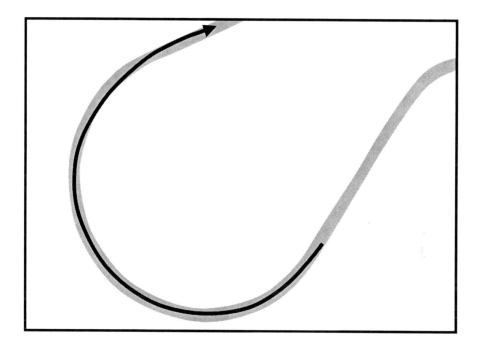

Also known as the "sweeper" or "rabbit ear", Turn 2 is a 200 degree left to right sweeper with a relatively flat camber and a steady uphill grade that surprisingly climbs more than sixty feet in elevation from corner entry to corner exit. This corner is an adhesion limits test for your tires and suspension as you hold your arc on an initial 450 foot radius corner. The corner apex is almost at the very end of the segment, as the radius of the corner shortens and then pinches in slightly, but materially, in the final third of its length.

Though a small subtlety, this shortening of the radius at corner exit makes any early apex a magnified mistake that will force the driver to lift throttle to avoid running off the left edge during track out if the tires are working at their limits, as they should be, coming through the middle corner section. So be patient and deliberate with your driving arc, which will allow you to transition from a maintenance throttle to a full WOT as you come across the very late apex point.

Get your peripheral vision working early and swivel your head to the right not later than mid corner to identify the apex point, so you do not get surprised being five feet too far to the left of the apex when you arrive. This will help you steer smoothly to the corner apex by following your line of sight, yet still track your driving line with peripheral vision. The right to left lateral inertia will throw you to the left edge of the surface rather quickly during corner exit, so as soon as you have your apex identified, get those eyes up and take in both the track out point and the corner entry for Turn 3.

You need to pick a reference point above the track surface for your track out point, as the actual surface of the left edge is not visible from the corner apex due to a small and subtle crown in the pavement as it follows the hillside topography. There can be a tendency to unwind the steering on track out a bit too quickly here. Recovery from an early apex in the corner at the end of the track out is complicated by the little crown or hill crest at the left edge, because it impairs the cornering grip of the car, presenting the possibility of either shooting cross track to the right or losing the rear with an over correction of too much steering input that does bite into the surface with the front, or dropping the front left off the surface because the front won't bite and you under steer or "push" through the steering input. Understanding that you have reduced recovery potential during track out for an early apex, and carrying high speed, you must hit the exit apex precisely, or slow down. Transition the car up the short straight from the left to the right edge. You have time to check your mirrors and gauges from track out to before you reach your braking point.

(**Beginner's note:** This is the ultimate in "tire talk" corners on street tires, and even DOT-R compounds. The driving line on this corner has more margin of safety than Turns 8 and 9, so you can push a little harder and still have some room for control recovery if you start to get loose, as long as you keep your driving line several feet inside the left edge of the track surface. You should have a long squealing transition here as you work the slip angles of the street tires and they deliver an increasingly sharp pitched howl at you. Do not panic and let off the gas because they begin to start making noise. Listen to the sound, and how it gradually changes as you approach the limits of adhesion. The pitch will alert you to when it is transitioning from working, to slipping, to sliding.

If you are not familiar with "tire speak" then you should get some skid pad time before running this, or any track circuit, close to the limits of tire adhesion. Each set of tires-they are all different-will talk to you and what they are saying will be most worthwhile to understand. And besides, the skid pad can be a lot of fun! The skid pad is where you can explore the limits of adhesion and the tendencies of your car to under steer or "push"-when the front wheels lose traction first- or over steer or become "loose" – when the rear wheels lose traction first – and how to regain control smoothly and quickly when they start to slide.

Most factory production cars, including high performance models, come to the buyer with under steer programmed into their handling characteristics. The simple reason for this is that for most street encounters with a driver who is not trained in performance driving, and that means almost everyone, under steer is thought by many to be the safer alternative to over steer to regaining control. The reason is that a common first reaction to loss of control by an untrained driver is to lift throttle. (Another is to crank even more turning input to the steering, but since the front wheels have already lost grip and the car is "pushing", sawing back and forth on the wheel does not help the car regain control, or necessarily lose it. It can make it worse when the tires do eventually regain grip if they are at full lock in a direction that you don't want to go!) In an under steering car this throttle lift will reduce velocity, and transfer more inertial force or weight over the front wheels, helping the tires to regain grip and thus give the driver control once more.

A reflexive lift of throttle on an over steering car can worsen the loss of control by lightening the rear even more, when there already is not enough grip, promoting the chance of a spin. Since the counter to this being "loose" in the rear is to apply throttle and apply counter steer, a very unnatural action that must be applied with a boxer's hand speed, it is not as safe a default reaction to expect untrained drivers to have.

Some cars with rear engine configurations will have a propensity to over steer because of the front/rear distribution of weight. If you have a rear or mid engine car, and you are not experienced in high performance driving with that type of vehicle, by all means coordinate with your track day sponsor to have an instructor who does, so you do not get surprised with a sudden swapping of the rear and front positions of the car in a high speed corner.)

The driving line for Turn 2 will depend on the car, suspension and type of tires, but generally speaking you want to avoid crowding the inside of the corner in the first three quarters of its length due to the diminishing radius finish and late apex. Try to hold the entry to the corner to the middle to 2/3 outside line, carry speed from the straight towards mid corner, then transition to a wide arc exit line and work a sweeping finish to the apex point that allows you to be accelerating out of the corner, without running off the left edge on track out. Be careful about going more than 2/3 of the track width towards the left edge as you can lose grip with surface debris.

You may want to draw your driving line by working back from the corner apex and track out point on the left edge of Turn 2, describing the longest radius arc that you can back to the mid corner section, so that you can then apply as much throttle as possible through and out of the turn, assuming you have a car that has enough power to break the grip of the tires along that line.

Examine the maximum velocity that you can carry into the turn from the medium straight between Turn 1 and Turn 2, and then you might try to meld or marry the two driving lines together in a mid corner transition segment that requires the minimum of modification to steering input or application of throttle.   If you have less power than required to break traction in the corner, you may consider adjusting the driving line to permit a shorter arc on the post mid corner section, so as to allow a longer and higher speed arc on the pre mid corner section, for the overall highest speed.

(**Advanced drivers:** Danny McKeever has a faster entry that does not load up the left front tire as much on entry, thus scrubbing speed. You make your corner turn in about one car width or slightly more from the position of the car on Page 36 to an entry apex that is about one car width inside the right edge, and ride the arc to the mid track to just outside mid track position between one third to one half of the way through the corner. This distributes load more evenly and allows higher speed, but it also requires feel for front to back balance and the ability to subtly adjust without losing control at the limits. Work this in careful increments of increased speed. If you do not understand exactly what your car is doing under these circumstances, don't do this.)

(**Beginner's note:** Turn 2 introduces you to something else that is notable about Big Willow, and that is deciphering the optimal driving line for *your* car. It will vary, sometimes noticeably, from the driving line of other cars. Accordingly, you have to be self disciplined to not fall into a habit of following the line of a car in front of you, because it is unlikely to be the right one for you. If your car is able to handle a tighter line, closer to the inside of the corner, at WOT, then that is a shorter distance and you should take it. What is more likely to be the case is that your driving speed is less than the capability of the car, and thus you take the tighter line. Practice taking the proper, higher speed line even though you are going slower. You will with time and experience begin to approach and enter the corner at higher speeds. As you do so you will eventually encounter the limits of adhesion of your tires, and thus will begin the process of adjusting your driving line to be able to handle that higher speed.

Typically, that will mean a larger turn radius or longer arc, thus moving the driving line farther towards the outside of the track surface, if that is safe, or determining that you have reached the safe limits of velocity in this turn for your car. You will not usually find yourself in a sweeper hugging the outside edge of the surface, even though it is the longest arc, as there are other factors that become relevant out there at the edge of the track surface. One is the dust and rubber marbles and other detritus that adversely impacts your grip, and another is the lack of room to lose even a touch of control and yet still recover without going off the track surface.)

Let's finish this turn with an emphasis on two points... surface condition and tire grip on corner exit of Turn 2. Because this is a diminishing radius corner at the apex, an "at the limits" grip can turn quickly into a loss of adhesion. This condition, combined with a left edge that is pinching in from left to right, a roll away of the camber, accumulated marbles and rubber, the probability of a warmer afternoon track surface (a common feature of afternoons in the Mojave Desert regions), and perhaps a "greasy" tires condition on your car, can all combine in small measures to give you less control than you had earlier in the day, or even the prior lap. An off track excursion here is not infrequently characterized with a roll of the vehicle. So dial down the aggressiveness and be safe.

Turn 3

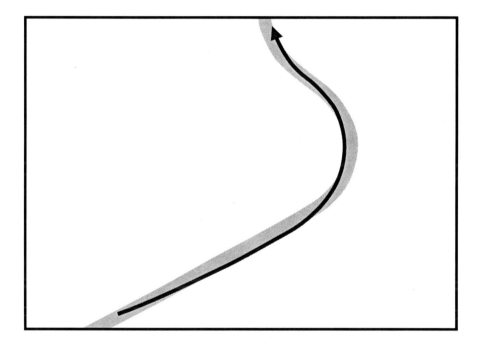

This is a right to left corner transitioning to a short but steep eighty foot hill climb, and from about a two foot positive camber, to flat to slightly negative camber just as you encounter a small crest at corner exit and track out from Turn 3 and entry to Turn 4. Your approach to Turn 3 is to straight brake, and do it hard, from the right edge and down shift, probably two gears, and make a *late* turn in. This section is one where you can lose a lot of time, but there is not a lot to be gained by hard charging into Turn 3 as it immediately transitions to the slowest and most technically complex corner on the circuit. Smoothness and clean technique to maximize your limited velocity, and best corner exit speed is now the change in theme from the squealing and roaring from Turn 1 to Turn 3.

(**Beginner's note:** Be ready for the rear of the car to become loose left to right with the combination of the little hill crest and falling away of the camber at Turn 3 corner exit, and to counter steer quickly to hold the car steady if necessary. Letting off the throttle here will only exacerbate the light tire grip and promote a spin (lift throttle over steer which is enhanced by the pitch forward of vehicle weight, and left to right inertia, and vertical inertia on the slope change, when power is reduced to the rear wheels). And getting on throttle hard can also promote a spin (throttle on over steer which is induced by breaking traction from too much power to the rear wheels). Accordingly, make the turn in to this corner late, and *squeeze* the throttle with smooth precision – consider using not just the ball of your foot but perhaps the flex of your toes for a finer tune pedal control – to keep weight on the rear, but not enough to break traction. You may also lightly unwind the steering just a touch to the right as you align for entry to Turn 4, to reduce the lateral inertial energy working against the rear as you crest, and leave more grip for acceleration.)

Many cars spin here fighting to move a couple of feet farther to the left of the track surface than they need to. Instead of doing that, as the rear settles down increase throttle and gently release the car to naturally drift to the right, directly into the "entry apex", and prepare to steer gently right as you enter the dual apex "Omega". You are not going to pass anyone on this short transition steeply up hill to Turn 4, even in a race, unless they were too aggressive and lost control exiting Turn 3. Don't be that driver! Keep control and be smoothly accelerating rather than lose time sliding around.

Turn 3 corner entry should be late.

Note camber flattens on Turn 3 corner exit.

Turn 3 lead car is quickly "loose" in corner exit and pointing at wall on left.

Prepare for the Unexpected

A few words about safely getting by a suddenly distressed car in front of you. This section of track at Willow Springs presents a good spot to remind ourselves that all of us are out on a track to have a good time as safely as possible. But sometimes events will unfold that are not on the menu of "good time", and you need to be prepared to deal with them.

Most of the occasions on track when a car gets into difficulty that presents a potential or actual risk to others, the corner workers at their flag stations and connected by their radio sets to each other will be signaling track conditions in front of you that allow you to take appropriate and safe measures to manage the hazard.

Know the flags!

Most events involving an off track excursion or other hazard transpire from start to finish in a matter of only a few seconds, and somewhere other than right in front of you. With typical track lengths of 2.5 to 3.5 miles and lap times of between

1:45 and 3:00 minutes, you often have an abundance of time and space to be warned and prepared. By the time you arrive at the scene, the car involved may already be back on track and on its way such that you never even see it before it reaches the track exit. Or the last wisps of dust and tire smoke are wafting away and the car is stationary. Visibility of track conditions at Big Willow are quite good, with few obstructions to your view and long stretches laid out before you. The basic blind spots are the exit of Turn 2 as you enter that sweeper, the back side of the Omega at Turn 4, the apex and track out of Turn 6 which are behind a hill crest, and the conclusion of Turn 9.

But eventually, and it could be your first day out or your fiftieth, somebody is going to "lose it" in front of you in close enough proximity that advance corner worker flag signals are not relevant.

You are on your own judgment and skill to avoid disaster, and it is on you immediately.

It could be a loss of control of that car. It could be the surprise of a part falling off such as a lug nut, exhaust pipe, body panel, even a drive shaft, or a fluid being discharged from a blown coolant hose or engine oil. It could be a small animal bolting across the track, or a plastic bag blowing on to your windshield. It could be you losing your brakes, or having other control problems. Your engine may quit, clutch pedal stick to the floor, or steering fail. All things mechanical can break, and many of them do break.

One recalls pulling up behind a car at an HPDE event at Big Willow, approaching Turn 7 at about 125 mph and preparing to pass on the left side. Another car was following a few lengths back. The overtaken driver was going about 115 mph, timely and clearly gave the point by signal to pass on his driver's side, and just as more throttle was applied and began to initiate a bit of steering to the left initiated to make the pass, a "marble" from the overtaken car's rear wheel and the size of a large olive ricocheted off the rear view mirror housing, through the window and into the throat of the driver in the overtaking car above the driving suit collar and beneath the lower edge of the helmet.

A "marble" is a gooey clump of molten tire rubber, often of the consistency of not quite done fudge brownie from the oven... and just as hot. They may shed directly from the tire of the car in front, or be picked up by a tire, spun around a few hundred or thousand times (picking up micro bits of grit, plastic and metal shavings) and then catapult away. Most of the time they fall harmlessly to the track surface. Occasionally they bounce off the hood, windscreen or roof of a following car.

Apart from the impact jolt into the throat, which fortunately was dissipated somewhat by the collision with the mirror housing, the goop immediately burned and fused to the skin. No time to lose concentration, and risk losing control with a jerk of steering or stomp on the brakes, or momentarily losing focus and striking the rear or side of the leading car or going off track. The decision was to keep both hands firmly on the wheel, complete the pass, exit the track after Turn 9, and have another driver peel off the congealed and then cooled rubber, apply the appropriate minimal first aid wash and disinfectant, slap a band-aid on, and then get back out there for some more fun. Since that date the decision has been to always wear a balaclava under the helmet, and keep the face shield lowered. And if that lesson was not clear enough, stopping a 1/4 inch pebble smack in the center of the helmet face shield at 120 mph in a formula car one spring day at another circuit was the exclamation point.

One could probably run this track 1,000 more times and never have that particular event happen again. But other things equally odd and challenging to your concentration *almost certainly will happen* during those 1,000 other runs. Deer, dogs, possum, raccoon, coyote, squirrel, jack rabbit and other creatures are not uncommon jaywalkers on many circuits. Wet leaves, pine needles, dust and grit, rubber marbles, not to mention oil, water, coolant, brake fluid, steering fluid... the possibilities of surprise challenge are without limit. You don't get to choose, you must be ready for anything. Every lap is new and different and you must be focused in your concentration without lapses.

If you are following another car, even at a distance of 20 or 30 car lengths, you should have them in your vision clearly as your head should be up. This Turn 3 at Willow Springs reflects a classic corner where as you are coming to the apex of the corner and preparing for your turn in to the Omega, you should be monitoring the car in front and aware of whether it has negotiated the track out to the slight hill crest and change in surface camber successfully. If that car in front has lost rear traction in a left to right slide, or even dropped one or more wheels off the edge, you have time to back off the throttle and give room and time for the events in front of you to unfold, including if necessary to slow down or stop or even deliberately leave the track surface should that be the safest alternative left available to you.

You should not assume that because the car in front of you has drifted off to the left that it is safe to pass on the right or that the other driver is even aware of your presence. The driver could easily "over correct" and swing the tail of the car hard around and then shoot directly cross track from left to right in front of you. Indeed it should be presumed that the driver ahead has his/her hands very full with the challenge of car control and has lost all focus on everything else.

One risk is that they could compound their track out error of running off the left edge or losing rear traction with an overcorrection that launches them across the track from left to right, hammering the throttle and taking a path to the right that could simply cause one of you to go nose first into the side of the other in a violent collision.

As the overtaking car it is your responsibility to manage a pass safely.

You have the advantage of being in control of your car and seeing everything in front of you, while the car in front of you does not. Accordingly, with your priority being safety, and not the achievement of your personal best lap time on this lap, *slow down.* This does not mean that you should slam on your brakes and create a second potential hazard to cars approaching from behind, and a compounding of the danger and complexity of safe passage. Rather, with the knowledge of who is behind you and how close from having checked your mirrors on approach to Turn 3 after exiting the Turn 2 sweeper in the "straight" between the second and third corners, you begin your safe evasion of the problem in front.

If the driver in front exhibits a controlled exit and slowing off track to the left, safely pull off line to the right and pass, then merge back on line to the right edge and set up for the entry to the Omega Corner.

If the driver in front is spinning on the track surface, apply brake smoothly and slow down while carefully watching the direction of his momentum and what the car is doing. If he/she is "both feet in" (clutch and brake pedals fully depressed) and sliding to the left or right edge, stay oriented to the opposite edge and manage your speed to be able to take safe evasive action if there is a sudden and unexpected change in the direction or dynamic of the car in front, such as a roll or flip or sudden regaining of traction so that you can stop without colliding.

You want to get safely by the event if you can, so that approaching cars from behind are not an additional danger to you or the car in trouble. Once you are past the event and out of immediate danger yourself, you can follow the directions of the corner workers, which may be a simple yellow flag caution, or a black flag to all drivers to come in to the pits under caution, or even a red flag to all drivers to come to a full and complete on course stop until directed to restart.

What a lot of your study to driving a course efficiently does is highlight the places where not only you might get into trouble, but where other drivers are likely to get into trouble and how and why. You should analyze what you ought to do as a driver should that trouble occur to you, so that you have prepared for it and can react quickly... there is no time for leisurely reflection in the midst of the challenge. You should know where the run off areas are, where the walls or other obstacles are. You should have already determined what you need to be doing and why and how before you ever get there. You should also have maintained sufficient track awareness that you know whether there are cars approaching from behind so that your recovery efforts are going to be among the safer options.

That preparation for what you are going to do if you get in trouble also helps you to understand what the likely dynamics of a car in front of you are going to be should it be in distress, and what is likely to transpire as the driver struggles for control, so you can act accordingly as the following car to avoid further mishap to either of you.

This should be a part of your preparation and study for driving every corner on every course before you strap in to your car to drive it. And then closely note in your orientation laps with your instructors, and in your own warm up laps, the action options and whether they match up to your expectations from your track map reviews, in car videos you have watched and discussions with other drivers. If the sponsor organization offers an orientation ride around the track for drivers, by all means do it. Even better, try to get the opportunity to walk or bicycle around the track.

A slow, close up look at the track will reveal subtle undulations, changes in camber, surface grip conditions, run off area characteristics and much more. If you can do it with four or five other drivers, you will pick up much valuable information during your conversation as you journey around the circuit. Don't forget to note not only what is on the track, but what is off it and within the possibility of being struck if you go on an off track excursion, and modify your behavior while driving accordingly.

Turn 4 - The "Omega"

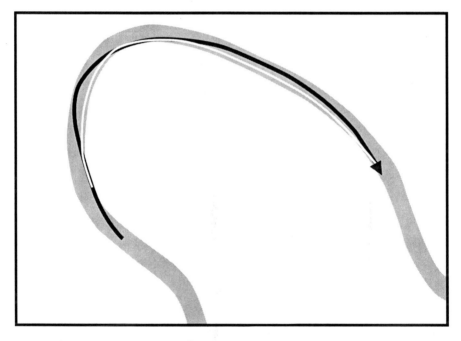

The "Omega" of Turn 4, below the balcony stands, is at the very highest elevation on the track, almost 160 feet above the lowest point. It provides a spectacular vista of the entire race course, though not one you can enjoy optimally when behind the wheel. An oddly shaped double apex, 210 degree corner, this Turn 4 "mushroom" has about as many differing ways to be approached as the famous story about how the blind men have differing ways to describe an elephant. And most of the approaches suffer from that same incompleteness of analysis. Everybody that drives the Omega has occasions they leave muttering "there has just got to be a faster way" to drive that corner. (Or is it just me?)

Part of the challenge is that the approach is steeply up hill, the mid corner section follows a short and tight uphill increasing radius corner entry, has a flat crest and extended or open "mushroom" shaped top, followed by a downhill and slightly off camber corner exit which you are completely blind to until you are upon it. And it is the slowest section of a very fast track, which probably enhances the feeling of driver impatience and frustration.

There are lots of different ways to make small mistakes in the Omega. Indeed it is common to make two or three self perceived errors, and heaven knows how many you don't realize, and just be sputtering at yourself as you rumble down the hill after corner exit and approach Turn 5. When you do seem to get it right you are so amazed that you are asking yourself "what was it that I did that time that was the key... how do I repeat it?"

(**Beginner's note:** It is not so much what you do to drive the Omega *fast*, as it is avoiding the things that cause you to drive it *slow*. This complex corner is more about not losing time than it is about gaining time. Knowing the limits of your car and being able to control it as you load and unload the suspension from side to side and front to back, both with steering and your throttle/brake, are what will navigate you through and out of the Omega, and get you that little bit of extra corner exit speed downhill towards Turn 5 that you crave.

This will take time to learn, so do not be impatient. Instead take the opportunity to observe and learn every time you go through the Omega how the car responds and you will gradually be able to understand through feel what is happening to the car and why, and your skills will improve at taking the car to the edge of control, and when you exceed the edge how to bring it back under control, safely. It should feel "smooth" even though the car is under strain at the limits to hold on to the surface. You want to be floating/gliding/slipping through this segment, not lurching and lunging from side to side or "porpoising" weight from front to rear. This is a corner that you will finesse, not pound, into submission.)

Driving Lines. If you take the car after the "entry apex" on a driving line deep and towards the left edge at the top of the Omega, a powerful car can effectively create a straighter and harder full throttle acceleration climb from the bottom of Turn 3 up the hill, through the entry apex on the right and to perhaps a car width from the top of the track, using its grip for the application of power and less for turning, then give a short throttle breathe or even stab on the brakes and turn sharply right to line up on the "exit apex", and if you are an advanced driver you can induce some rotation and utilize left foot brake technique. (But do be careful about getting a tangle of "happy feet" if you are not accomplished with the technique, because it has to be quick and precise here). This "high line" approach for a powerful car allows the driver to unwind the steering more than possible had you taken the tighter driving line, and squeeze back on the throttle harder to get that brute power to the wheels across the exit apex point on the right edge of the track. This pulls you wide to the left of the track surface on exit from Turn 4, opens up the angle down the hill for approach to Turn 5 and makes a slightly straighter and longer section, both up into and then down out of the Omega, and for some powerful cars a faster one.

It also creates a tighter radius turn at the top... and thus a slower one... so you have a compromise on driving line similar to one encountered on sharp "fish hook" shaped hairpin turns followed by long straights. Because it is a slower corner the intermediate driver may hasten the transition by choosing to deliberately induce a rotation or yaw of the nose of the car by flicking the wheel and giving a little extra squirt of throttle to break traction in the rear and then catch it with counter steer. Not a drift, but a quick realignment of the angle of attack.

Is the trade off of a slower top turn offset by carrying more speed up and into the turn, and the opportunity to be straighter and harder on throttle on exit? Not necessarily.

A lesser powered car with better cornering characteristics may benefit from a tighter entry apex line because it does not have the tires working at their maximum grip accelerating up the hill through the entry apex... there is no added speed reward in that instance because the car just does not have the power to accelerate up hill rapidly enough... so that car may apply the unused and available grip instead for turning and shorten the distance traveled through the Omega to get through the corner in the shortest possible time... with more distance from the left edge driving line of the powerful car, clipping the exit apex with perhaps a slightly wider track out angle to the driving line, but again with less power available and the ability to carve a tighter radius turn during track out than the powerful car has, even though the lesser powered car is under WOT at corner exit.

There is room to the left exiting the Omega for both driving lines to accelerate and track out wide to hook up power to the rear tires.

The infinite number of exit apex angles you can choose that trade off the arc of the radius for maximum available power to the wheels, and the change from up to level to down, and on-off camber, can put any power car in a position where it will exceed the grip limits of its tires and slide or spin, so no matter what you are driving, the Omega corner will keep both the higher and lower horse-power cars searching for the optimal driving line.

Since there are a wide variety of types of cars on the track at one time, and even similar cars are rarely set up the same, following the line of another car through this corner can be sheer folly. What works great for the Corvette is unlikely to be ideal for the Porsche 996 or BMW E36. For the higher horsepower cars in particular the deep approach at the top reduces the power on over steer that the fall away camber at corner exit induces when you take a tighter line close to the right edge, with a smaller turn radius, as you are dropping the right foot to the floor in your enthusiasm to rocket down the hill. The definitive answer to how to take the Omega fast is… "it just depends on everything".

(**Beginner's note:** This corner is a balancing act of extracting every last bit of grip from your tires in a combination of acceleration and turning… which explains why it can feel like the corner is different every time you hurtle through it… it IS different unless you take it precisely the same way every time. Even if you do take it on the same precise line, given the dynamic change in the handling of the car as the tires warm or get "greasy", the fuel load and thus weight changes, and the driver concentration and focus varies, and the angle of attack and velocity change as does the radius of the corner exit if you are off just a tiny bit on your line or braking on corner entry. This little corner is a Rubik's Cube puzzle and it merits your getting there early and walking every step of it before you strap in and ride through it. Think about what you and your car are doing and why, have a plan of attack, execute it, then re-evaluate and adjust the plan to improve.)

What is a great lessen to take away from driving the Omega is that *it illuminates what is the truth about every turn on a track...* it is different every time you encounter it. What distinguishes the Omega from other turns is that the difference is imperceptible and in most cases inconsequential in those other turns. But it is there. The Omega helps you to work on enhancing your awareness of what your car is doing, why, and what you as the pilot can do to adjust, and that can pay rewards everywhere you drive.

The exit from Turn 4 commences an increasingly fast section of the circuit, and thus the reward to a smooth and fast corner exit is carried with rapid acceleration all the way down the hill through Turn 5, over the crest of Turn 6, and ultimately the approach to Turn 9. The transition from Turn 4 to Turn 5 is thus extremely important to developing a fast lap time, even though it is not a super fast segment itself, based on your corner exit speed from Turn 5.

Smoothly roll on the power so as not to unbalance the car while accelerating and in most cars up shift one gear as you get to your track out point from Turn 4 and set up for entry to Turn 5. Check your mirrors. If your car is not powerful enough to compel you to lift throttle or to brake before Turn 5, then the maximization of corner exit speed from Turn 4 becomes all the more important.

Transition from exit of turn 3 to entry of Turn 4. Though pointed mid track, the car is drifting slightly from left to right towards the corner entry apex.

Note how drift has taken car to entry apex for Turn 4. The apex for the powerful car driving line does not touch the right edge of the surface.

Turn 5

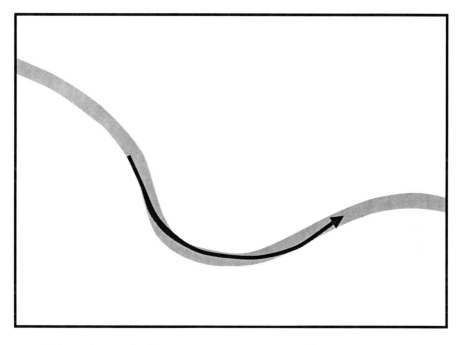

The downhill segment exiting from Turn 4 will drop you almost seventy feet of elevation to corner entry, in a left to right transition for set up to entry to Turn 5. The high horsepower cars will be going very fast with the assistance of the downhill slope and need to apply some brake before corner entry, which should be from the right edge of the track surface, putting some weight on the front right tire to help it take a set on turn in. Work the geometry of this turn carefully, as being precisely aligned parallel with the right edge at your turn in point is probably to be aligned too far to the right. Try to make it a few degrees to the left of parallel, but without "crabbing" left into or crowding into the corner, inducing an early turn in to the corner that will make you apex too soon.

A subtlety to the entry to Turn 5 is the downhill left to right Omega post exit apex bend. If you are tempted to hug the right berm too soon you may drift too far left for optimal corner entry to Turn 5. Some cars will therefore be better suited to hold out more towards to the left edge on track out from Turn 4 so that they can manage to be properly aligned with the right edge approach to Turn 5 as mentioned above. Also, a car that needs to apply a touch of braking before turn in to Turn 5 will benefit from this slightly opened approach, because the driver can then manage the touch of braking, possibly with the left foot, into a short segment that is straight, rather than with steering applied, as he transitions from the left to right bend into the right to left corner entry. Turn 5 is a medium speed, high lateral G force, turn from right to left, with about two feet of negative camber working from the left to the right edge of the track surface, but with an increasing radius, so you may have a bit more room to go faster on corner entry than your initial reaction.

(**Beginner's note:** The off camber corner is going to move you farther to the right edge than a flat corner taken at the same velocity, but if you look at the directions of your inertial momentum and your driving line you will see that it is not pushing you directly sideways, but angled forward slightly, between the driving line and the slope of the track surface, giving you more margin than you might have thought for both track out and recovery if you need it.)

Gradually experiment with earlier application of power through this corner to pick up more speed to climb the hill to Turn 6. Again, the challenge is in the balance of power and suspension/grip, and developing the highest velocity possible to carry you out of the corner and up the rise to Turn 6. Here there are potential gains available from the unused grip in your tires in the early phase of the corner that you will benefit from all the way to and potentially through Turn 8.

Turn 4 exit apex leading to downhill run into Turn 5

Set up for Turn 5 is along stripes at right edge.

Turn 5 apex. Note how camber falls away to right side of track. Stay on throttle to keep the rear drive wheels planted and the car accelerating.

Turn 6

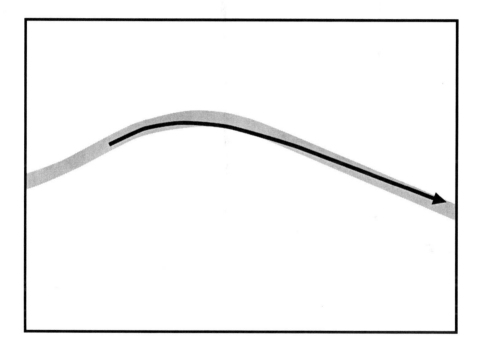

As you exit Turn 5, keep your eyes focused up hill and looking to mark the apex to Turn 6. You cannot actually see the corner apex from your position below as it lies beyond and to the right of the visible hill crest track surface, and a couple of feet in elevation lower. So you need to pick a spot or angle to where the apex lies to the right of the farthest right edge of the surface that is then visible to you. If you pick the edge of what you see from below... you are increasing the likelihood that you will early apex and run off the track surface during the corner exit.

Smoothly up shift on track out from Turn 5 and in a high power car work your way to the left of the track surface uphill and under full throttle so that you may increase the arc of the corner radius on the left to right Turn 6. It is possible that you will be able to move all the way to the left edge in the distance between Turn 5 exit and Turn 6 entry, but some cars won't be able to manage a full transition. Thus you need to determine based on your speed and handling limits how far left you must move, and can move, to generate the fastest speed through Turn 6 that allows you to meet your corner apex point.

The larger arc radius will promote a later apex and higher maximum speed through and exiting the corner. If you cannot carry maximum speed out of Turn 5 and into Turn 6 without running out of room on track out from Turn 6, then you need to adjust your driving line out of Turn 5 to do so, as maximizing Turn 6 exit speed is more important than Turn 5 exit speed.

In the process of expanding the arc of the corner radius for Turn 6 you will also reduce the severity of the unbalancing effect of the angled crest at the top of the left to right Turn 6, and the flat to slightly off camber downhill track out driving line that could cause you to slide off the left edge of the track surface. You will lose much of the grip on the right side of the car as you crest the hill, and some faster or stiffer chassis cars will actually lift the front right wheel completely off the track surface. A lower power car may elect to track farther out to the right of the surface on exit from Turn 5, then stay closer to the center or even right edge before making a corner entry into and through Turn 6, as it will not have enough power to throw the car off the left edge of the surface after cresting the hill on track out from the corner, and this shorter route through the corner will be faster for their car.

(Beginner's note: On no account should you be shifting gears in corners, and certainly not in this corner which coincides with an angular hill crest. Finish your up shift after Turn 5 and be back on power before you crest, or wait on the up shift until you have passed the hill crest and settled the right side and rear of the car on track out.)

As you come over the hill crest in Turn 6 the left edge comes at you very rapidly, because the geometry of the corner is still closing in from the left. It is not uncommon for a driver, especially someone new to this track, to drop the two left wheels just off the track surface. This usually comes from the natural, but in this case mistaken, instinct to assume the corner apex is at the crest of the hill, when in fact it is quite a few feet after the crest. Fortunately at this writing the dirt is smooth and the lip of the track surface very short, so the undercarriage will not be pounded and you can carefully work your way back on the track without ripping your exhaust off the car if you keep your calm. But when you go and take your warm up lap, take note of what the track condition is at that time for the fifty to one hundred or so yards you might have to glide after dropping two wheels, and then ease yourself back on track from.

(**Beginner's note:** If you find yourself with lateral momentum potentially sufficient to carry your two left wheels off track, you have a split second decision, to determine whether you have enough grip to apply a touch more steering sufficient to keep the wheels on the surface... or don't you? If you don't and you apply steering you have some risk of either spinning or sliding all four wheels off, both more serious consequences.

A better approach may be to smoothly lift off throttle, do not touch the brake, and straighten out the wheel and roll very briefly with two wheels off and two wheels on. If you apply power you will have little grip on the dirt and much on the blacktop, and you will have a control problem, especially if you steer back to the right and the rear hooks up under power and shoots you across the track and over the other side. So just ease your way back onto all four wheels on the surface under light power, and when firmly four wheels on the asphalt apply significant power and continue on your way. If you have picked up gravel and dirt in your tires, stay off the primary driving line until it is shaken off. If you go all four wheels off, hold the steering straight and gradually come to a complete stop. And look for the corner worker to signal you it is safe to re-enter the track surface.) Most track rules require a car that has gone two or more wheels off to pull into the pit area for a safety inspection to make sure that any pebbles that may have lodged between the tire and the rim, or brake pads and rotors, are removed before you continue your session.

Turn 6. Note apex is beyond and below hill crest, with positive camber up the slope.

Turn 6. Note how camber rolls away and track slopes downhill following corner apex.

Turn 6 corner exit on left edge, then move slightly right to position for entry to Turn 7.

Turn 7

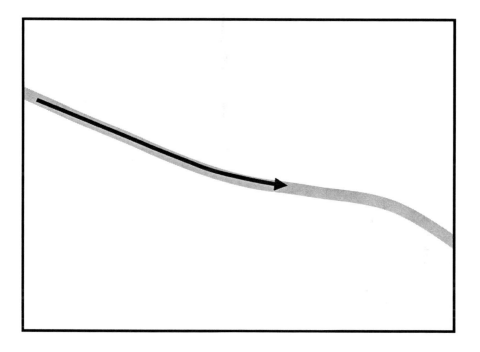

On exit from Turn 6 stay down on full throttle, track out to the left edge and then ease your way about a car width or slightly more to the right of the left edge of the track to "straighten out" the 10 degree right to left kink that is Turn 7, and proceed through it WOT. Follow the left edge and prepare for entry to Turn 8. From the crest at Turn 6 you will be dropping almost sixty feet of elevation to the corner apex of Turn 7.

(**Beginner's note:** Use this long "straight" section to check your mirrors, gauges, and concentrate on picking your best corner entry and driving line.)

Approach to Turn 7 to position for entry to Turn 8 from left edge.

Turn 8

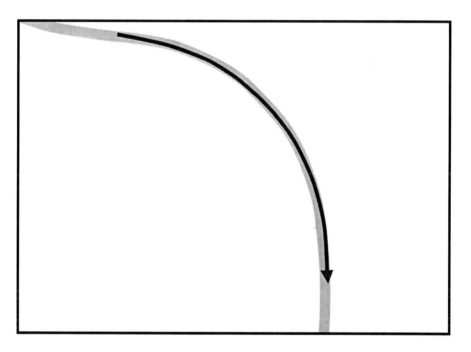

This corner is a high speed left to right increasing (900 foot radius) sweeper that can be driven in a properly prepared car by a well skilled driver in excess of 125 mph. A lot slower is advised for the overwhelming majority of us. The driving line is outside the midline for most cars. The surface is a predominantly flat camber. The inside three to five feet of the track surface are frequently compromised with sand and silt from the prevailing breeze, which adversely impacts tire adhesion, and should influence your selection of corner "apex" and move it inside the right edge of the surface.

There is a short "straight" connector between the exit of Turn 8 and the beginning of Turn 9, and if you have ample power you want to describe the longest radius you can from the far left edge Turn 8 entry to exit into the straight connector. If you cannot exceed your grip limits on that driving line, then you may shorten the radius of the turn to travel a shorter distance to the connector. If you can exceed your grip limits on that driving line... well, you just have to slow down!

The ticklish part is the corner entry where the arc radius is the tightest, and whether at the maximum velocity you have been able to generate roaring down the hill from the exit of Turn 6, and the rate of acceleration that your car is delivering you can keep that speed/acceleration rate relative to the increasing arc radius. Remember, your tires only have so much grip to give. You can use it turning, you can use it accelerating, and you can use it while doing both. But if you lose it at high speed as you will in Turn 8, you have a very significant car control challenge.

If you have a car that has more than enough grip relative to the speed it can carry at WOT, then Turn 8 for your car is not so tough, you just keep the pedal down and carve the correct driving line through it. But if your car has more power, speed, acceleration than the suspension and tires can hold while under WOT and turning, you have to reduce throttle and shed some of that power to the wheels before entry to the corner, then get back on the throttle with gradual increasing power to take advantage of the increasing radius to accelerate through the turn and into the connector, balancing along the edge of maximum speed and control. For the advanced driver, if you simply maintain speed at what you were carrying into corner entry, you may be leaving a lot of lap time here. This section of the course begins to flatten out, with perhaps an eight foot elevation drop from Turn 7 to the exit of Turn 8.

(**Beginner's note:** This corner is not unlike Turn 2 as an adhesion test... but much faster. It is not a place to first be learning high speed grip limits on tires, as the consequences of going on an off track excursion at triple digit speeds from Turn 8 are harsh. Use discretion and good judgment. The more tire grip you use in acceleration, the less tire grip is left for cornering. As you are in a corner and inertial force will throw you off the track, give priority to the cornering component of grip utilization.)

If you do have the power to exceed grip limits even when describing the widest arc you can drive through Turn 8, and you can squeeze even a bit more speed accelerating into the straight connector at the end of Turn 8, be mindful of the need to get your braking and adjustment of corner entry speed accomplished before setting your corner entry from the left edge of the "straight" connector to Turn 9.

The connector is a good place for another mirror and gauge check.

Position for corner entry to Turn 8.

Mid corner driving line in Turn 8. Leave room on left for safety.

Exit from Turn 8 to connector for entry to Turn 9.

Entry to Turn 9.

Mid corner in Turn 9, searching for apex. Note skid marks going off track to the left.

Turn 9. If this apex were any later it would already be tomorrow. Put right front wheel on small "dip" along right edge at apex of corner.

Turn 9

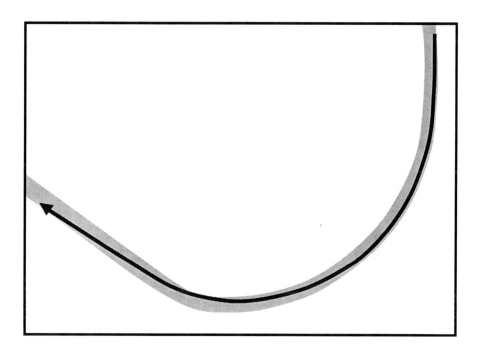

If only one corner could be described as having the potential for being "evil", this corner is it. Many of the more difficult turns on road courses have famous and even colorful names. The Canada Corner and the Kink at Road America, the Andretti Hairpin or perhaps the Corkscrew at Laguna Seca, the Bus Stop at Buttonwillow, etc. This corner does not need a name... the road course cognoscenti all will recognize the simple reference of "Turn 9" to be Big Willow's most challenging corner, potentially one of the toughest of them all.

The initial approach to Turn 9 is presented near or over 120 mph in many cars, in some cars well over. Novices should be going **much** slower. The driver is well advised to study the map geometry of this turn carefully, and to be very patient in driving it. Work up your speed in this turn in very gradual and deliberately calculated increments.

The 600 foot corner entry radius appears to be wide and generous, and at *entry* it is. But the driver has just finished taking the increasing 900 foot radius Turn 8 and accelerated into the straight connector segment leading to Turn 9, and no matter how often one drives this transition it somehow psychologically always seems to be a surprise at how **suddenly** Turn 9 clamps down, in no small measure from the difficulty many drivers have in being able to recognize the location of the corner apex.

The driver is now confronted with a decreasing radius turn, which tightens as if into a sharp spiral at corner exit, so that a slight miscalculation of driving line or speed leading to an early corner apex will direct the car off track at very high speed, unless the driver brakes or lifts throttle, either of which in themselves may further unbalance the car and promote a loss of control.

The challenge is compounded by the fact that the track camber is flat to slightly negative from corner apex to corner exit, and slightly downhill by perhaps six to eight feet from corner entry through corner exit. The apex is very hard to locate visually on the flat desert even if you swivel your head sharply and look far ahead for it, something tough to do when you are going into a decreasing radius corner that fast.

The high speed through the exit of Turn 8 and potentially increased in the straight connector to 135 + mph has to be shed, and the challenge is that it occurs just as you need to begin feeding in steering from left to right, which reduces the braking capacity of the tires as they are using grip to turn the car. But *if you are a racer* should you brake too much or too early as you approach entry to Turn 9, you lose speed that you could have carried through.

Since you are not a racer do not fall into that trap. Brake too early and get it done before corner entry to Turn 9! Do it smoothly and do not upset the balance of the car....so a bit early and gently.

With the radius constantly diminishing, demanding ever more tire grip to hold the car on line, and then abruptly tightening at the very end of the corner, with the car positioned on the outside left edge of the track surface, there is little room to recover before going off track, as the typical technique of straightening out the steering a touch to regain grip is compromised by your relative position on the track.

Too much greed for speed can be severely punished. If you straighten steering you run off the track into the desert. The under steering car will just lose front grip and push nose first into the desert, and the over steering car will waggle its tail loose in to the dirt, forfeit almost all grip at that moment, and send the driver spinning backwards and sideways off the track into the desert. If you take your eye off the driving line of a diminishing radius corner searching for the corner apex while still pushing the limits of adhesion at triple digit speed you can easily drift off surface into the desert.

None of these are particularly attractive options; please review them again if you have doubts and note especially the part common to all four that you are "into the desert" at triple digit speed.

To provide yourself some safety margin, you need to pull in the geometry of your driving line a few feet towards the center from the left edge, and leave the "banzai" mentality locked in a vault. As the corner leads to the half mile long front straight, braking or lifting throttle or early apexing are mistakes that have large negative consequences, just as the reward for carrying high speed through and out of Turn 9 is given great reward. Though that may be technically correct, accept the emphasis that safety outweighs speed for all corners, and no exceptions ever for this one.

For the racer in competition, this is a gut tightening encounter every single lap. For the track day enthusiast who needs to drive home in the car he or she brought to the track, this is the turn to be most wary of, but it should not be a problem if you use good judgment. (It is said that good judgment is something you learn about two nanoseconds after you recognize that you have exercised bad judgment. But let us avoid that revelation on this turn, and prepare now). The edge between a skillfully negotiated corner and a rollover exit can be thin here. This is not a turn where "luck" should be in the vocabulary, because you should not be pushing it close enough to the edge of control to call "luck" into relevance. You may rely on judgment and skill; luck is always too busy helping someone elsewhere to save you from Turn 9.

(**Beginner's note:** This corner provides as much adrenaline rush as any in high performance driving and racing, but also real danger. *So take this one easy as a matter of course, always.* Unless it is your business to push the envelope as a professional driver on this turn, there is no rational reason to do it here.

Favor the outside left of the track surface, with a sizeable bit of room from the edge for safety margin. At least a car width to start, but do not go as far to the right as mid track. Advanced drivers can get closer, but even they should consider leaving two to three feet of margin here. Keep your head up and swiveled only slightly to the right to be looking into the turn, so you can accurately monitor your margin away from the left edge of the track, follow the edge through the early phase of the turn and wait... wait... wait on making your move to the right until you see the water tower in the distance align itself with the center of your hood. (I use the water tower because it seems the easiest, but pick any reliable landmark that works for you.) Then turn your head further right to fix the location of the corner apex which should now become visible clearly where the drainage pipe goes under the track and there is a break in the curb, and make a smooth carve into the corner not by making a sharp steering input, but by letting your hands follow your eyes and flow smoothly. As you begin to track towards the apex, feed more throttle to the car if you can keep the drive wheels gripping, and the front wheels on the driving line to the corner.

Here is where Danny McKeever has a very useful "survival kit" tool as he calls it, for drivers at all skill levels. Where is your car positioned as the curb begins on the right edge? If you are mid track you are flowing on the right line. If you are inside of that line you may run out of paved surface on the left during track out... so slow down now!

Unlike the first part of Turn 9, you now should be looking with your head deliberately turned to the right, not straight ahead, to identify the apex. Leave some "extra" grip in your car to allow the hands to follow the eyes and describe the driving line towards the apex when it comes into view, but don't be "turning in" or cutting to the corner apex, and do not be running at the limit of adhesion to the spot where you first recognize the apex point... as then it will be too late to brake or lift throttle and still make the apex or keep the car on track. So here is the fun observation for turning to the corner apex at Turn 9: you don't. It doesn't really happen that way. One guides the car through the corner apex all the way back from corner entry without a demonstrable turn in "move". Taken correctly this corner has the driver with "quiet" hands.

The tangle of skid marks in Turn 9 are proof enough that a lot of people get it wrong, and some of those are from drivers and cars well beyond the capabilities that most of us will ever have.

The track out from Turn 9 will put you on the extreme left edge of the track surface at WOT, which means many cars with experienced drivers will be entering the front straight at 100+ mph. (That includes some momentum racers like the Spec Miatas because they have had all the time and track they need running down hill from Turn 6 to build up that speed, and it is not uncommon for good drivers in a Miata to run up behind a moderate driver in a Corvette that passed them in Turn 7 by the time they both reach the exit of Turn 9!)

Transition smoothly across the track to the right edge and proceed at full throttle down the half mile length of the front straight, past the start finish line, and into Turn 1. Again, check your mirrors and gauges, and then be looking far ahead to pick your braking and turn in points, and scan for cars entering the track on the left.

Track out to left edge on corner exit. Note car entering the track exit lane.

Track exit lane immediately following corner exit from Turn 9.

Track Exit

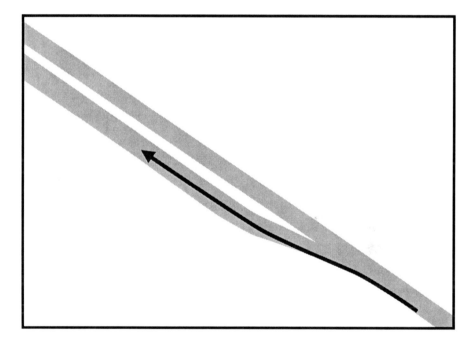

The exit is at the beginning of the front straight. That presents a potential problem in that the edge of control speed required for a fast gallop down the front straight is inconsistent with a smooth and leisurely transition off the left edge of the track to the exit lane, which is also along the preferred driving line.

This is further complicated by the fact that the classic signal for track exit is a raised arm out the window by the driver... which is hard to see by a pursuing car in a left to right corner, especially one as challenging as Turn 9 where a lot more focus is likely to be on what the driver is confronting and less on the car ahead preparing to exit. And, frankly, taking one hand off the steering wheel to deliver a signal that you are exiting while you are also going 100 mph in a corner is not a comfortable or advisable thing to do.

Accordingly, be sure to check your mirror in the connector straight section between Turn 8 and Turn 9, and if there is nobody in sight behind you, you can let up on the throttle a touch, and stay left on the surface, give the signal as you pass the corner apex and ease left off the track. (Always give the signal whether you think there is anybody behind you or not... you might be wrong).

If there is a car behind you and you know you are going to be exiting, you have a couple of choices. If the car is close or may safely pass before Turn 9, give the exit track signal, and perhaps a point by to the inside, lift throttle to facilitate a faster and cleaner pass by the pursuing car, and then follow the same procedure described above.

If the car as it moves abreast of you (not when it is directly behind you) is not close enough to pass but is within line of sight and will close on you as you exit, lessen the possibility of confusion and give the track exit signal in the connector section, perhaps lightly touch the brake with your left foot a couple of times to draw his attention to your car and your upraised arm, then proceed with both hands on the steering wheel briskly through the corner. Put the left arm back out the window as you approach the track exit. You will probably be going close to 90 mph as you merge off track, so as soon as you are moving to the off track surface, get your arm back inside and on the steering wheel and slow down in a safe manner, so that as you approach the turn in to the paddock you are easily down to 5 mph.

(Beginner's note: The car behind you may be exiting also, so do not brake too hard going into the exit lane and risk having a following car run up your tail pipe. The exit lane is long and straight and wide, so just pick a driving line and stick to it, and apply steady brake and down shifts into the hot pit area between the track walls. No passing should be made in the exit lane, but leave room for it in case the following car misjudges closure rates and still has clearance to avoid you on either side.)

The Mid Corner Challenge of Big Willow

Interestingly, many tracks do not have turns that emphasize skill in mid corner driving. Corner exit speed on all tracks is always a priority, especially corners that precede long straights, usually followed in priority by corner entry speed. Skillful braking to optimally put the car at the proper speed at precisely the proper spot for initiating corner entry may be next in importance. The time spent in mid corner sections on most tracks is very short in distance and limited in duration, lower in speed, and the consequences of mistakes there are usually much worse than the small advantages to be gained, (they almost always compromise the first priority of corner exit speed) so we don't necessarily work on the mid corner skill sets until a bit lower on our long list of areas to improve. But Big Willow uniquely has several turns that give significant rewards to mid corner driving ability, and Turns 2, 8 and 9 highlight this distinctive feature of the track.

(**Beginner's note:** The mid corner driving challenges of Turns 2, 8 and 9 are all uniquely different. Turn 2 is more of a sustained velocity corner with the nuance of a significant climb in elevation that does not appear as significant as it is, Turn 8 is a balance of acceleration under cornering through an increasing radius, and Turn 9 is a balance of deceleration/maintenance throttle under cornering through a decreasing radius, downhill corner, with a sudden "pinch" and camber change at the apex through exit from the corner. Each is at triple digit speeds. Study the track map for all the corners and think about what you will be doing before you drive the circuit. Take an orientation ride with an instructor before you drive the track yourself if you can arrange it. Most of the high performance driving education ("HPDE") clubs will provide instruction and orientation rides for first time drivers at Big Willow for little or no additional charge.)

Distinguishing Characteristics

Turn 1 introduces the driver and car to what Big Willow is all about... speed in corners. While geometrically and conceptually simple and straightforward, the negotiation of corners at such high speed is anything but simple. Picking the inception of your braking and turn in points, achieving optimal velocity, and still maintaining adhesion of the tires is a delicate and sensitive affair in all high performance driving.

You need to anticipate the impact of delay in response of the car to your inputs, and your own reaction time when calculating where to initiate your braking and steering inputs. Commanding the car with early control inputs, many of which are subtle, rather than "busy hands" reactive response, will be a safer approach. Initiating braking earlier and more smoothly is a way to ease into the corners and not upset balance. The real prospect of losing adhesion at such high speeds puts a premium on car control for the intermediate and advanced drivers, not often encountered on most road courses.

Big Willow and its nine corners throws that challenge at you time after time... Turns 1, 2, 7, 8 and 9 are all in the realm of potential 100 mph + corners for the high horsepower cars. Now here is the real kick in the pants... those same turns are in the realm of potential 100 mph + corners for "momentum" racers like the Spec Miata, and when superbly driven those cars with excellent suspensions can be going faster through those segments than high power brutes and registering some very low lap times. (For most cars Turn 7, a 10 degree kink, is really not a corner at all, in the same way that Laguna Seca's Turn 7, the "Rahal Straight", is not a corner.) But just because you can get a car going that fast does not mean it will take the corner, either with you or any other driver behind the wheel. More importantly, just because somebody else can do it in the same kind of car does not mean that you can.

(**Beginner's note:** While a golfer may exhibit some dismay at striking the ball out of bounds due to a lack of concentration or timing, collateral consequences are limited in most cases to a couple of bucks for the ball and potentially a dent or chip in something in its flight path or the landing zone. Relative to other objects likely to be encountered, the ball itself is rather impervious to physical distress. In performance driving you "are the ball", and the ramifications of a lack of concentration or timing that takes you out of bounds can forcefully ricochet you off a concrete wall or turn your car upside down at more than 100 mph. You are not impervious to physical distress and the damage to the car is probably going to cost more to repair than the cost to replace a golf ball, so respect the difference in the game, the true meaning of "distress" in each instance, and approach these types of velocities and challenges carefully and in modestly applied increments. You may in golf, however, go ahead and swing as hard as you can, just in case you hit it.)

Turn 2 exit. Note ditch area to left off the track surface.

The Supercar Owner

If you have an exotic like a Lamborghini, Ferrari, Porsche Carrera GT, Ford GT or other powerful stock or modified car that is street legal but capable of exceptional speed, Big Willow can be an excellent track to legally experience some of the straight line capability of the car in a reasonably safe and legal environment. You can exceed twice the legal highway speed limit on two or three sections of the course in those cars, and marvel thereafter at the engineering they deliver every time you take a casual drive even though you are cruising under the legal speed limit on highways and country roads. Most of the run off areas are groomed and flat, there are very few walls and obstacles to hit if you do go off track (a big factor with an expensive toy), and you don't have to be pushing adhesion and handling limits of either the car or yourself in the high speed turns to still be enjoying the heck out of the experience, or keeping up with the pack.

Most clubs and HPDE sponsors will separate their outings into three or even four groups, so one that is averaging a speed that you are comfortable with is almost certainly available, as are instructors to show you the driving line and help improve your skills throughout the day. There is something about having a super car and not having had the experience of driving it fast that rubs a nerve for many people, (mostly those that do not own one and pepper you with questions about whether you have driven on a race track with yours!) but they don't know what to do about it. A day at Big Willow in your fast exotic can be an answer for that. It may be the one and only day you take it to a track, but it will almost certainly be a joyous and unforgettable one.

Conclusion

There you have one lap of a very fast race track, where the apparent simplicity of the nine turn layout is overwhelmed by the subtlety of skill needed to command a car safely at high speeds at the limits of adhesion the suspension and tires can give. There is relatively little wear and tear on the gear box, or demand for a novice to have polished heel/toe downshifting skills, and the brakes only have two hard braking segments before turns 1 and 3 on this track.

Here the engines are working hard, the cooling systems are being tested (Coolant, Oil, Power Steering), and the suspension tuning and tires challenged. Above all else, this track tests the skills of the driver in keeping his/her car just on the safe side of the edge of control.

For the more casual driver who is not approaching the "edge" of control, the track is a very fun and safe, yet comparatively high speed romp where the technical difficulties are pretty much limited to getting around the slowest corner of the Omega, and being conservative in Turn 9.

For the professional and advanced skill level amateur drivers, Big Willow offers challenges in car control, mid corner driving and recovery skills rarely encountered elsewhere so consistently at such prodigious speeds, paired with one of the most technically intriguing corner puzzles of the double apex Omega.

With its close proximity to the City of Los Angeles, high speeds, technically complex Omega and sobering challenge of Turn 9, it is no wonder that Big Willow has been and continues to be such a popular road course for driving enthusiasts of all skill levels.

Reflect for just a moment, that all of the driving decisions described above, and more, will transpire in a single lap, compressed into about one minute and forty seconds, as contrasted to the considerably longer time that it took you to read a summary description. And will be repeated ten to twelve times in a single session of HPDE driving, without pause or respite physically, mentally or emotionally. And you will have four, five or even six sessions available to you in a single day of driving.

This means that you need to be aware not only of track conditions, your car and your tires, but of yourself as a driver. How is your physical stamina, your ability to mentally focus and maintain concentration? If you feel that you are physically or mentally slipping at all, get off the track and take a break, or pack it up for the day. Snow skiers know that it is pushing to get in that "one last run of the day" where the accidents happen. Take it easy and take it smart, and come back to enjoy another fun day of HPDE.

Closing Note on Driving Lines

There is much more to determining the optimal driving line (and braking inception points, corner turn in points, corner apex points, track out points, etc.) than just an exercise in geometry on a flat road map. Because that is only the starting place for developing the "best" driving line for you.

Track conditions will influence your evaluation of the line to take. What is the weather? Is it cold or warm? Is it dry, humid or even wet? What is the condition of the surface in any given location of the track? Is the camber positive, negative or neutral? Is the surface ascending or descending?

The car you are driving will influence your evaluation of the line to take. What type of car are you driving, how heavy is it, what is the weight balance of the car, where are the drive wheels, what type of suspension (springs/dampers/control arms/ camber adjustments/anti sway bars/strut towers/ bushings), what type of tire and tire compound, inflation pressure, tire size, how much horsepower/ torque, what type of slip differential, what type and size of brakes/brake fluid/pads do you have?

Who is driving will influence the evaluation of the line to take. What is your experience, what are your skill sets, how familiar are you with the particular track, what is your physical condition, are you mentally sharp and focused today?

Then you have the subtlety of Big Willow that a couple of the turns have apex points that are not at the inside edge of the surface, such as the corner exit apex for Turn 2, the corner entry apex for Turn 4, and corner entry apex for Turn 8. Turn in for corner exit apex at Turn 4 is a full car width from the left edge at the top of the Omega....and there is no definitive corner turn in for Turn 9 at all!

Now add to this the fact that many of these factors are variables that change throughout the course of the day, indeed some of them through the course of a single session. Accordingly the purpose of the driving lines presented in this guide are to give a general orientation for you to become familiar with the track and then promptly develop your own before you begin to push your personal envelope that day. Obviously, novices should not be "pushing" anything other than the priority of having a fun safe day by staying well under the limits of performance for the track, the car, and themselves. This guide is not written to teach driving. There are many other excellent books that address technique, and excellent driving and racing schools. I encourage you to explore both to the fullest of your ability to do so, as they will enhance both your safety and enjoyment of high performance driving.

Track Checklist

Minimum Required of All Run Groups

❏ Helmet. Snell rated SA 2000 or better. Motorcycle helmets are not acceptable.

❏ Tech Inspection form

❏ Car Numbers – required on both sides of the car and rear, a minimum of eight inches high – this can be with blue painter's masking tape – any self adhering but removable and re usable numbers, vinyl or magnetic, must not peel off at high speed

❏ Tow hook installed (preferred) or tow point clearly established

❏ Long sleeve cotton shirt and full waist to ankle cotton pants (Cotton or Nomex clothing ONLY. No leather or synthetics allowed. This includes underwear).

❏ Closed toe shoes, preferably with a thinner sole for improved pedal feel, cotton socks

❏ Torque wrench, lug nut socket that fits your wheels

❏ Tire pressure gauge

Highly Recommended for Intermediate and Advanced Groups

❏ Driving Suit of not less than two layers, preferably three layers, fire resistant Nomex

❏ Race Driving gloves

❏ Race Driving shoes

❏ Nomex socks, undergarments, balaclava
❏ Face shield for helmet
❏ Fire Extinguisher, fixed within reach of seated and belted driver
❏ Neck brace, collar or Hans Device
❏ Racing seat or bucket
❏ Properly installed harness system of five points or more, three inch or more belt width.

Optional Supplies

For the Driver:

❏ Drinking water or electrolyte drinks. No alcohol drinks permitted on track site at any time. No smoking anywhere in the garage or pit areas.
❏ Hat – for Sun
❏ Sunglasses
❏ Sun Screen
❏ Folding chair
❏ EZ-UP Canopy
❏ Hand Soap/clean wipes
❏ Ice chest
❏ First aid kit
❏ Map/directions/phone number of hotel
❏ Map/directions/phone number of track
❏ Camera
❏ Camcorder/mount

For the Car:

❏ Extra Brake pads
❏ Brake fluid – one bottle
❏ Engine Oil – two quarts

- ❏ Power steering fluid – one bottle
- ❏ Coolant-Radiator- one gallon
- ❏ Distilled Water – Radiator- one gallon
- ❏ Duct tape – one roll
- ❏ Painter's tape – one roll
- ❏ Glass cleaner – You will kill some bugs on your way to the track. You may collect rubber streaks from "marbles" and more bugs on the track
- ❏ Brake Bleeder line and collector bottle
- ❏ Hose Clamps- assorted sizes
- ❏ Zip ties – one dozen
- ❏ Work gloves, heat resistant
- ❏ Jack – as light a weight yet strong as you can find
- ❏ Two foot long wood 2" X 4" stud
- ❏ Jack stands (2) minimum
- ❏ Jumper Cables or Jump starter box
- ❏ Service manual
- ❏ Other tools (sockets, wrenches, pliers, screwdrivers, allen keys...)
- ❏ Utility knife, multipurpose tool, scissors
- ❏ Grease
- ❏ Paper Towels – one roll
- ❏ Clean rags - six
- ❏ Trash bags - two
- ❏ Run Flat aerosol cans
- ❏ Tie Wraps
- ❏ Stopwatch
- ❏ Race tires and wheels, one set
- ❏ Spare tire
- ❏ Tire pyrometer
- ❏ Flashlight
- ❏ Funnel for oil
- ❏ Gloves – disposable

Tech Inspection Form

Driver:_____ Date:_____

Make:_____Model:_____

Year:_____ Color:_____Stock or Modified:_____

Note: If you are self-teching your car, it is your obligation to physically check every item on this form. Do not assume your lugs are tight, re-torque them to make sure. This checklist is for your safety and the safety of the others on the track with you, and should not be dismissed as a formality. If the item is "good" mark with a check. If it is not, write "NO" and call it to the attention of the registrar, and support will be found to assist you to address the issue. After teching your car, you must sign the bottom of the form (in both places if you're self teching), which indicates that you have, in good faith, checked every item on this form. Please bring this form with you to the track, or you'll have to do a new tech at the track before you will be allowed on the track, possibly missing your first run group.

WHEEL and TIRES
Street Tires:
❑ More than 2/32" of tread?
Race Tires:
❑ Good condition/no cording?
❑ Cuts or other defects?
❑ All lugs present and torqued?
❑ Hub/Center-caps removed?

ENGINE
❑ Any fluid leaks?
❑ Wires/hoses secured ?
❑ Throttle return springs tight?
❑ Radiator overflow OK?
❑ Battery properly secured?
❑ Battery terminals covered
    (rubber boots / duct tape OK)?
❑ Fluid lines OK?

BRAKES
❑ Pedal pressure firm?
❑ Fluid level correct?
❑ Lines OK?
❑ Brakes lights working?
❑ Pads more than 5mm?
❑ Rotors OK (no cracks, etc.)?

STEERING & SUSPENSION
❑ Wheel bearings OK (no play)?
❑ Steering tight?

BODY
❑ Gas cap OK?
❑ Body panels secure?

SAFETY EQUIPMENT
❑ Helmet approved?
    (Snell 2000 or newer, M or SA)
❑ Seats secure?
❑ Long sleeve cotton shirt?
❑ Closed-toed shoes?
❑ Seatbelts properly installed?

APPROVED SEATBELTS
The following systems are approved:
(Please check one)
❑ OEM 3-Point
❑ 5 or 6-Point
4-Point*
*All 4-Point systems must pass
 fech at the event.
*4-Point Belts inspected by:_____

Note: Mark each line with a check (✓) if that item is OK; write "NO" if that item is not OK.

Print Name: _____ Signature: _____

Dedication

This book is dedicated to the many people that this adventure in high performance driving has brought me together with, past-present-future, and that I would never have otherwise met. The fraternity of drivers at HPDE has been steadfastly friendly and supportive in these early years, with helpful advice in learning courses and driving, shouldering jacks and pushing cars on and off trailers, even sharing parts and tools when necessary. All with a genuine shared enthusiasm for the sport, and a concern for the safety and well being of each other on and off the track. I hope with this effort to give back to our growing community a resource that will encourage safety, responsibility and development of skills so that all involved, both experienced and novice, will stay safe and well as they pursue their passion for driving.

Acknowledgement

Danny McKeever and Fast Lane Racing School, for reviewing this text and suggesting exquisitely subtle insights and perspectives on driving lines and techniques for this very wonderful, and incredibly fast, race track. Danny is a "teacher of teachers", and ten minutes of his undivided attention on driving is probably filled with more valuable information than ten hours in the classroom with most instructors. His great competency as a driver, love of sharing the art of driving, and patient manner, have made him the master of this circuit for better than forty years. Danny ran his first race on Big Willow in 1963, and has been thinking about how to drive it longer than almost anyone has been racing, and longer than quite a few readers have been alive. His contributions to my introduction to driving this circuit have not only improved my understanding of the track, but proven conclusively that, as with most circuits, one approaches a "whole 'nuther level" of considerations and required skill sets as the edge of the performance envelope is encountered. Though the location of that edge is different for each of us, as long as Danny enjoys and wants to teach his art, you will be well served to seek him out if you seriously want to learn and improve, and especially if you want to do it at Big Willow.

Photo courtesy of Sammy Davis Photography–Los Angeles, CA

About the Author

Edwin Reeser is just another one of the millions of motorsports enthusiasts, who devotes entirely too much time, energy and funds to the passion of high performance driving. You too will have reached this point when 1) you won't supersize your french fries order for a few additional pennies but think nothing of spending another $1,500 for a high flow exhaust, 2) accept the logic of the racer's adage "if you are under control you are not going fast enough", and 3) have no emotional reaction to substantial cosmetic or mechanical damage to your car, when you formerly would have had hysterical upset from a door ding, other than concern over how long will it take before you can get back on the track.

Other Race Track Attack Guides from Sericin Publishing released in 2010:

Laguna Seca - Monterey, California

Buttonwillow Raceway Park - Race #13 Clockwise - Buttonwillow, California

Auto Club Speedway - Auto Competition Course with "Roval" - Fontana, California

Reno Fernley Raceway Park - Configuration A - Fernley, Nevada

Thunderhill Raceway Park, Willows, California

Track guides in preparation for future release:

Sears Point Raceway, Sonoma, California

Las Vegas Motor Speedway, Las Vegas, Nevada

Spring Mountain Motor Sports Ranch, Pahrump, Nevada

Willow Springs International Motorsports Park - Streets of Willow, Rosamond, California

For more information go to:
www.RaceTrackGuides.com

Breinigsville, PA USA
02 August 2010
242859BV00002B/5/P